# 50 habits of successful networkers

Timea Kadar

FRANCIS COOPER PUBLICATIONS

*To all the wonderful people who I met or will meet at networking events.*

Hi, I'm Timea, the author of this book. I want to help you make the most out of networking.

Like many others, I used to think that networking means being in a crowded room with strangers and talking about yourself.

Until I understood that networking means building meaningful relationships.

Having attended hundreds of networking events and having met thousands of people, I have seen what the most successful networkers do.

I founded London Business Society and in partnership with London Connector and its Founder Duccio Zambrini, we organise and host over 100 premium networking events a year in prestigious venues.

At our events, people build human-to-human relationships, which grow to collaborations, business and even friendships.

In this book, I showcase 50 habits that each successful networker has and follows. Short explanations are followed by practical, easy-to-follow tips to make these a habit.

I'd like to thank Ildiko Torma-Kadar for the wonderful hand drawn illustrations, and Akos Bard for some of the quotes.

If you're new to networking, and you don't know how to get started...
If you are an introvert, or overwhelmed by meeting a lot of people...
If you don't know how to introduce yourself...
If you have been networking for a while without success...
If you love networking...

...this book is for you. Browse it, dip into it, read a few tips and try them in practice.
If you have any questions, concerns, complaints, or any other tips to share, please get in touch: tk@franciscooper.com

See you soon.

Timea

## 1. Good networkers don't keep score.

If you want to see an immediate return on networking, it takes your focus from what really matters. You will stop attending a group before the balance would turn 'positive'.

You won't notice important things like a friendship being born, or a connection who would be very useful for someone in your network.

You will be so stressed to make a return on each event, each meeting, and 1-2-1, that you will miss the real fun of it: belonging to a community where you, as a person matter.

Where you're being taken care of. Where you're listened to and supported when you need it. And where you are cherished and celebrated when you succeed.

Networking is a marathon and not a race. Don't keep scores and you'll win.

## How to make it a habit

I suggest you keep building relationships within the same circle - event series, organisations, group, or with a person - for a year (unless you dislike it after the first few occasions). This seems to be a long time, but remember that you don't meet them every day or week.

Make a commitment to regularly keeping in touch for a year, without stressing about having a client or income from the group. After about a year it's worth reviewing how you contributed to them, and what you got out of it.

If you found anything positive in the balance (even if it's just being with like-minded people), go on. If not, it's time to give it up.

## 2. Look for people with the same core values, not the same industry

'*Which industries are attendees coming from to this event?*' - sounds a frequent question.

And it's not necessarily the right one.

First of all, it's not always possible to know in advance.

More importantly, instead of the industries, always look for the core values of the group, as it also determines the core values of the attendees.

If those align with yours, you're more likely to build good relationships.

At our events, we have people who value human-to-human connections, which then lead to business. As all our attendees align with this core value, we can guarantee our guests a very supportive and committed community.

**How to make it a habit**

First of all, it's good to identify your own core values: these are principles that are non-negotiable in how you operate, how you live. Knowing these is crucial if you want to find people who have similar ones.

Many event organisers post about their past events on social media. Check the photos, the vibe, the comments. Follow them to see what kind of other events they host. Contact them and ask them what their goals, and their core values are.

You can also click 'Attend' at events published on LinkedIn. You can see other people who plan to attend, and check their profiles, their activities.

Joining Meetup groups and their events is another good way of checking who else is going (or says they are going). But the real test is to attend events, feel the vibe, talk to the host, talk to other attendees.

3. Don't think of people as leads. But where they can lead you.

I'm often asked who is attending our networking events. People want to guess how relevant the attendees are to their business.

Networking is not performance marketing, and a networking event is not a lead generation tool. (There are other marketing techniques for that.)

It's impossible to know who will actually be there. And even if they are your ideal clients, they won't necessarily come to the event being ready to buy what you offer.

It's not about who is gonna be there, but who they know. Who they can connect you with after they learn more about you.

It's about what they know. You can get access to a lot of insider information, hints, and tips, you wouldn't find on the net.

And likewise, you can also refer them to your connections and share knowledge to support them.

When you go to your next event, keep an open mind and connect with like-minded people. Don't think of them as leads, but as people who can lead you to the right people.

**How to make it a habit**

Make a habit of asking connections not only about their work, but
- what they do in their free time
- where they spend their holiday
- what their background is: where they studied, what they did before what they do now

- their family, what they do, where they study
- if they have pets
- any fun facts

Obviously, you don't want to make it an interrogation, and you might need many meetings to find out more. But soon enough you will have a bigger picture of their network you can tap into.

## 4. It's not about the number of people but the quality of conversations.

Some networkers worry about the size of the event they attend. They are keen to talk to many others.

Spending a few minutes with everyone leads to superficial talks. What kind of impact will it have on the other person?

I have seen community leaders like Gabriella Ferenczi (Language Professionals Networking Event) and Martin Zeman (Business Leaders' Family) building a curated group of quality people over the years.

They have kept running their monthly events no matter what happened in the world, and no matter what the size of the actual event was. I have some of the best memories, and best connections from these groups.

## How to make it a habit

Aim at talking to 'only' a few people at an event. Stay longer with those you have a good talk with, regardless of their 'potential'. Concentrate on the quality of the people and the conversations, and give them quality time and attention.

## 5. It's not what the person does, but who the person knows.

Some networkers quickly move on if the other person doesn't fit the profile of their prospect.

Remember that networking is never about selling to the other attendees. It's about getting access to their network, knowledge, and experience.

It's about who they connect you with. What they can teach you. What kind of information they can share with you.

It's not only about what they actually do, but who - and what - they know.

**How to make it a habit**

Ask the person what kind of networking events they attend. This will give you an idea of their connections, and can give you inspiration for new networking opportunities.

You can ask them right away if they can invite you or if you can go along with them to a group they recommend - and you like too.

## 6. The best icebreaker is honesty.

If you're embarrassed to start a conversation...
If you're an introvert...
If you are not good with icebreakers...
...use honesty.

Instead of trying to pretend to be the wittiest person in the room (you probably still are!), say that you are an introvert.

**How to make it a habit**

Test a few 'icebreakers' you can always use.
*"How do you know the organiser?"*
*"Is it your first time here?"*
Or you can say:
*"I am not really good with these icebreakers, are you?"*
*"I'm not very good with networking, I'm quite an introvert. What about you?"*

Honesty will break the ice more than anything. You'll both be relieved, and the other person might tell you they feel the same. Do you need a better icebreaker?

## 7. Showing interest in people works better than any pitch.

You might be anxious about your pitch, and how to talk about your business.

While it's a good idea to work on your pitch, giving people your genuine attention is more memorable than any rehearsed line.

**How to make it a habit**

Instead of the usual questions, concentrate on what they say and - like a good reporter - ask more details about it.
- Why they chose the profession they pursue.
- What happened with the client they talk about.
- What they are proud of.
- What they would do differently.

Going into more details gives you a better picture of them, and they will feel it was a great conversation, and that you are a good listener.

8. Tell me about your favourite client, and I will know you much better than if you tell me what you do.

If you ask people what they do, they will tell you their title, their profession, or even a few words about what it means.

This way you will hear very similar things from people in a similar business/profession, and it will be very hard to refer them to others.

Learning more about their clients, you'll understand right away what problems they solve, how they solve it, and what kind of people their clients are. You'll even see if their clients could be good connections for you.

**How to make it a habit**

Ask the other person about their favourite client (and not an ideal client which most people can't specify properly), and a wonderful story will come to life.

Likewise, if you're asked about what you do, say that the best is to bring an example and talk about your favourite client. (Be prepared with a few client stories and choose the most relevant one.)

## 9. Be in it to win it.

Have you ever hesitated to sign up for an event? Or cancelled one in the last minute thinking it was not worth attending?

Ian Abrahams from Treacle Factory shared the story of his mum always saying 'You have to be in it to win it.'

This inspired him to attend events even if he sometimes didn't feel like, and this brought him a lot of great connections and business.

This has become my inspiration too when I try to decide to go to attend an event or not. You never know what an event would bring you or would have brought to you unless you're in it.

You never know what a relationship could grow to unless you invest in it, and get to know the other better.

## How to make it a habit

It's impossible to be everywhere with everybody, but without investing your time and effort in building relationships, you won't be able to take out anything.

Commit to a few events or meetings with people (it can be a group of like-minded people you pull together). It's better to have a few groups and attend regularly than jumping on every opportunity.

Put it in the diary and don't consider it optional. Make an effort not to cancel whatever happens (except for obvious reasons).

## 10. Not all puzzles fit together.

Have you ever tried to put together a puzzle?
Isn't it fascinating that a piece fits only in one
place, and doesn't fit in many others?

It's the same with people. Not everybody is a
good fit for you. And you're not a good fit for
everybody.

If you feel that the chemistry is not the best
with someone at a networking event, it doesn't
mean that it's your fault. Or their fault.

It's ok to move on if you feel the other person is
not for you. Or if they don't share the same
core values.

**How to make it a habit**

Have your 'exit sentence' prepared so that you
don't stay longer out of politeness.

Simply say something like: '*It was great to chat, I look around to see who else is here.*'

11. People will forget your pitch. But they won't forget if you made them feel interesting.

Always ask the other person to introduce themselves first.

It's quite easy as most people like talking about themselves. It helps you get an idea about them and find out how you can make your introduction more relevant.

Keep your pitch relevant and succinct. And then ask more questions.

It gives you even more information about the person. And it makes them feel interesting.

**How to make it a habit**

As you hear the other person talking, make some positive affirmations connected with a question (obviously when you're genuinely interested) like

*"That's a very good tip, could you explain it a bit more?"*

*"That's a fantastic achievement, I'm sure you have put a lot of effort into it. How long did it take to do that?"*

If they start talking about their family, ask the names of their children or pets.

This makes them talk about more personal things, and have a better memory of the conversation with you. (Plus you can make a huge impression on them next time you ask about the kids by their names.)

## 12. Junior people are the leaders of tomorrow.

I always encourage students and junior people to attend networking events. Some of them tell me that when some of the attendees realise they are juniors they quickly move on.

Apart from the fact that it's rude, it's also stupid.

Junior people are the leaders of tomorrow, and in a few years, they will be decision-makers at leading companies.

And even if not, you make the first networking event of a young person pleasant and a good memory.

In our community, there are wonderful entrepreneurs who are happy to support and mentor juniors. Like Miles Phillips, Marketing Strategist or Sarah Clay, LinkedIn Trainer who generously offered to share their expertise with my interns.

**How to make a habit**

Young people often don't have the courage to start a conversation and are easily talked over when in a group.

Make it a habit to give them the imaginary 'mic' asking them about their studies, assignment, dissertation, research. Ask them why they chose that topic and what their next plans are.
Offer them help and a future 1-2-1 if they want to hear more about your profession, or anything you're strong at.

## 13. You have to open a lot of chests to find treasure.

You might feel you are going to a lot of networking events, connect with new people, do everything as recommended, and nothing comes out of it.

Not all your contacts will turn into an opportunity of any kind. Not right away. Or not at all.

But the treasure is always there waiting for you in networking if you don't give up.

**How to make it habit**

Organise short 20-min 1-2-1s with people you met. This gives both of you a good opportunity to explore a bit more about each other and find synergies.

If both of you feel so, you can agree to attend another networking event together, or have another 1-2-1.

You can also organise group catch up meetings with 3-4 new connections, which is an efficient and quick way of finding out more about each other.

14. Connect two people who are a good fit, and both of them will be grateful to you.

When talking to people at a networking event, don't only think about why it would be good to connect with them.

Think of who you could connect them with.

If you think this way, you can create a lot more connections, not just for yourself, but for others too.

As a result, two people will be grateful to you and want to give back to you.

**How to make it a habit**

Ask any of these questions from the person:

- *"Who is an ideal introduction to you?"*
- *"If I could introduce you to anybody, who would that be?"*
- *"Who do you want to meet here?"*

Try to think if you know someone (probably right at the same event) who could be a good match.

## 15. Networking in a hurry to save time will waste a lot of your time.

There are people who are desperate to 'work the room' at an event.

While they speak to someone they are already looking at who to talk to next. They freak out if they can't talk to everybody or if there are not enough people at the event. They invested time and money into the evening, so they want to make the most out of it.

But unfortunately, the opposite happens. A lot of quick, superficial conversations make no impression on others, and in fact, no connections will be made.

**How to make it a habit**
The best is to talk to fewer people and spend as much time as it feels good for both of you.

If you're a good fit, and it feels great to talk, don't worry about 'wasting time' because in fact, it has a much higher return.

When you attend an event, aim at talking to 4-5 people longer, and if you can make more conversations after those, it's a plus. Organise a group meeting with a few people who you enjoy being with rather than spreading yourself thin.

16. Turn away from people who never say '*it's your turn*' when talking to you.

I don't decide who to talk to again based on their industry or company size.

It's more important for me to share the same - or similar - core values.

It's a huge red flag for me if the person talks a lot about themselves, and doesn't ask about me.

You don't have to be a networking guru to be curious about another person.

People who are not curious about others, are not for me. And generally, they are not ideal networkers.

## How to make it a habit

If the person you are talking to never asks anything about you, or you feel like they don't pay attention, simply move on.

If you support someone a couple of times, and when you reach out, they disappear, simply move on. There are so many other people.

## 17. Dress comfortably, arrive early, and drink responsibly.

Check and follow the dress code of the event, but always make sure your clothes are not only stylish but also comfortable. If you feel a piece of clothing is too tight, too short or uncomfortable in any way, it takes your focus from the event and the people, and you won't enjoy it.

Arriving earlier at an event gives you an opportunity to make yourself familiar with the venue. You can talk to other early birds before the crowd arrives, and welcome those who arrive later.

It's tempting to switch off with a few drinks, but a networking event is still a professional environment and you don't want to make a bad impression. Have a drink, enjoy the conversations, but it's probably not the best time to let your hair down.

18. Looking for potential clients during a networking event is like looking for gold during a hiking tour. You won't find it, but miss the whole fun along the way.

If you look for your next client at a networking event, you become stressed about it.

You are unable to enjoy the conversations, and don't concentrate on people who are not 'prey-material'.

You miss the whole fun of it, and eventually, you won't get a client either because nobody wants to feel like a prey. Enjoy the talks, the environment, the food and drinks. Have fun and if on top of it, you meet a prospect, even better!

**How to make it a habit**

Rather than aiming at meeting prospects and potentially having a good time, switch the perspective. Aim at having a good time, and potentially meeting valuable connections. Someone who has a good time, and enjoys life attracts attention. Organise meetings with your connections to follow up while doing something fun you're both interested in: netwalking, attending a conference, doing some sport, walking the dog, visiting an exhibition.

## 19. Everybody has something somebody else would be happy with.

*'But what could I give to others?'* - I hear this question many times, especially from junior people and new business owners.

The truth is that everybody can give value to others. Everybody can give attention, recognition, and positive reviews. Everybody can support others on social media.

Unless you're a newborn baby, you have friends, family, teachers, neighbours who could be good connections for others.

Everybody has a specialist knowledge or experience in certain topics that could be relevant to others.

And finally, as you start networking and get to know people, you can connect them with each other.

**How to make it a habit**

Stop saying: *"I don't know anybody. What could I give to others?"*

Always think bigger than your direct connections. You might know introducers who could lead you to a person the other wants to connect with.

If someone helped you and you want to give back, but don't know anybody they are looking for:
- You can post about their request, or send it to some of your network, or share it in a group.
- You can give them a testimonial or a positive review.

- You can support their social media posts, events, activities.

They will appreciate the effort.

20. Growing your network is like growing a tree. It takes a lot of time and patience, but it will reach much higher than you and keeps bringing fruits.

There are people who attend a networking event and then come back: *'This wasn't too good, I haven't met anybody useful.'*

While it might be the case, it's not the reason not to go to networking events.

It's a fact that it takes time to build connections and a reliable network. You have to be prepared to have some failures too.

You meet some takers, you waste some of your time.

But once your network grows, it will reach higher and farther than you can ever imagine. You get help from the most surprising sources.

Whenever you need something, you have a bunch of people on the rescue. You have someone who knows you at every event.

And people keep recommending you to others.

**How to make it a habit**

To grow that 'tree' dedicate half of your networking time to follow up 1-2-1s, messages, introductions, and only the other half making new connections.

The best is to schedule regular catch up meetings with your network. It doesn't always have to be a 1-2-1. You can meet as a small group on a regular basis and share what you're

working on, and who you are looking to
connect with.

21. Connect with people you enjoy being with. It might or might not lead to business, but either way, you have fun.

When you decide on who to talk more to, don't decide based on industry or company size.

If you enjoy being with that person and talking to them, if you share the same core values, you can't lose.

**How to make it a habit**

Build relationships with valuable, fun people regardless of what they do. And even if there's no business out of it, you have fun.

22. If we both give value to each other, both of us will be richer. If we both wait until the other person makes the first move, we'll have nothing.

Being suspicious and cautious doesn't help build relationships.

Some people wait until the other person introduces them to someone. Until the other person opens up their little black book. Until the other person makes the first move.

If both parties keep everything to themselves, it leads to scarcity, and none of them gets anything out of it.

On the other hand, if both of you open up, and go above and beyond to help, it leads to abundance and a great relationship.

**How to make it a habit**

Instead of saying *"What I do"* say *"What I do for you"*. Make the first step, make an introduction, recommend them to someone or publish a post about them.

People are sometimes surprised when you first ask them, *'What can I do for you?' 'How can I help you?'* Then it teaches them to do the same.

23. Algorithms can change, social media channels can be down, websites can be hacked, but your network will be there for you, no matter what.

LinkedIn, Instagram, WhatsApp can be down.

Social media channels can change the way they show your content to followers.

You could be forced to stay at home, not to meet others.

What will never change is the power of your network.

The people you could call any time when you need help.

People who have your back when you feel you can't do more.

Connections who cheer for you and celebrate with you as you succeed.

**How to make it habit**

Apart from growing your follower count and posting on social media, make sure you take care of your real-life connections too.

Reach out randomly to ask how they are. Meet them from time to time in person. Support them on social media, and in messages when they share updates.

You'll get back a lot more, regardless of what's happening in the digital or real world.

## 24. Be the person whose name others love to see on their phones when you're calling.

Have you thought about what people think when your name appears on their phones as you call them? Or when they have a new email from you?

Do they say "*I will answer later*", or even worse, "*Not, again!*"?

Or do they get back to you with priority?

It depends much more on you than on them.

If you have gone out of your way to support them, if you always share relevant information with them, people will be happy to see your name pop up.

I have had several junior colleagues who go above and beyond to help me, and who I get back right away if they need anything.

**How to make it a habit**

Make yourself a priority for others to get in touch by making them a priority first.

The best time to start this is when you don't need anything from them. (Reaching out with a compliment AND a request is not a genuine compliment.)

Dedicate time regularly to recognising your connections, and showing care (sending a message to ask if you can help if you heard they are sick, offering support if they lost their job etc.)

## 25. Talk less to be remembered more

Going on and on with a pitch puts off people, and they stop listening.

Even if you have the 'mic', keep your pitch to the point.

Use plain words.
Use. Short. Sentences.
You'll be remembered more.

**How to make it a habit**

Write your pitch and break every long sentence to shorter ones. Each sentence should say one thing.

Instead of: I'm the co-founder of a XYZ company, we help THEM and THEM with THIS and THIS.

Say: *"I'm the co-founder of a X company. We help Y with THIS."*

It's much easier to follow and remember, and you won't mumble.

## 26. Be relevant to be memorable

If you meet someone, let the other person introduce themselves first.

Pay full attention to them, and find points that resonate with you.

Make your intro relevant to them, as we tend to remember more what is relevant to us.

Always focus on one area you do, the one you want to be remembered for in that situation.

Be as relevant as you can and you'll be remembered more.

**How to make this a habit**

Prepare a 'pitch-bank' which includes all the aspects of your experience and expertise. Based on what the other person said, choose something that is relevant to their background, something you think will click well. And don't talk about anything else.

## 27. Cooperation over competition takes both of you farther

If you follow a protective policy, your focus is on scarcity. Hiding, protecting, excluding - a lot of energy spent on things that don't grow anything.

On the other hand, if you focus on collaborations, and growing the other person, your focus is on abundance.

It's not hard to guess which one results in more success.

One of the best things we have done was partnering with Duccio Zambrini from London Connector, who would normally be a competitor.

Instead of running our events as competitors, we bring together our members and guests making it beneficial for everyone.

And we welcome other organisations to collaborate with us based on mutually agreed benefits.

**How to make it a habit**

Instead of solely looking for clients, look for strategic partnerships and collaborations.

If you find someone with the same core values, targeting the same audience but with a service that compliments yours - or see any other mutual benefits, - start talking.

The best is to start with a pilot and see how you work together.

The key to collaborations is that you both put in the same level of effort and have the same level of gain.

You want the other to succeed more than you and this way, both of you rock.

## 28. Take my money but leave my connections.

If I had to choose between giving away my money or my connections, I'd choose the earlier without thinking.

I can always earn more money, but I can't buy connections.

Those relationships took years to build and thanks to their support I can be more successful.

**How to make it a habit**

Networking is not something you do seasonally whenever you have time, or when you need new clients.

There might be periods when you are overwhelmed and can't attend events, but even then keep doing at least online meetings with your connections, or with a group of like-minded people. Never stop networking.

## 29. The most important networking lesson is to listen.

You might have heard this tip several times, and still, listening is sometimes hard.

It's not only waiting for your turn in silence but actively listening without thinking of what you're going to say.

**How to make it a habit**

Listen to what words people use, the emotions they express, and their body language.

Ask questions to clarify certain areas or to get more specific information.

Don't interrupt them, and pause for a while even when they seem to be finished. Many times people share gold when they go beyond what they planned to share. Information is power, and you don't get it unless you listen.

When it's your turn, you can refer back to what they said, and later on, you can connect with them easier.

## 30. Not the loudest person is the one who is heard

Standing out in the noise is a constant challenge.

Unless you're ready to give the stage to someone and focus your full attention on them.

Recognising their successes, asking questions, showing empathy, and caring.

This makes them want to find out more about you and is a much better strategy than being louder than others.

**How to make it a habit**

If you're standing in a circle of people where someone doesn't want to let the 'mic' go, stop them, and ask someone else who hasn't said anything to introduce themselves.

If you know someone who seems to be too shy, underestimating their influence, make a post about them and invite others to support the post if they know the person.

If you are a quiet type, who is intimidated to talk in front of a lot of people, talk to people in 1-2-1s and say honestly, that you prefer it this way.

You can also ask the host of the event or a confident attendee to introduce you to others.

Never be ashamed of being quiet or shy, it's a quality and nothing to be ashamed of.

# 31. Results sell you more than fluffy words

When you talk about what you do, talk about the outcome of your work.

If possible, support it with facts, if not, be very specific about what 'success' meant in that situation.

The outcome you deliver sells you more than describing what you do (and it's also easier for the other person to remember when they want to introduce you to someone.)

## How to make it a habit

When you prepare your pitch, try to find supporting evidence to justify your statements. Anybody can say 'they care', ' they do quality work', but how can you prove it?

Show results you achieved for your clients, reviews, feedback. Don't be afraid to use this as part of your pitch.

It's NOT bragging but helping them understand how you add value.

## 32. People forgive mistakes, but they won't forget dishonesty

Mistakes happen. Trying to pretend they didn't happen, or blaming others doesn't take you anywhere, and puts people off.

You can double-book a meeting, forget to get back to someone, or even make a mistake in your work.

**How to make it a habit**

A genuine apology almost always works, and people forgive you.

Take the blame even if it was not directly your fault, but somebody from your team.

Offer compensation if you can, and then you can both move on.

## 33. People bin flyers, but they keep memories

You can hand out flyers at an event (or leave them on the tables and chairs.)

Some people might pick these up, but more of them will end up in a bin.

Creating a positive experience for them, however, results in great memories that stay with them.

**How to make it a habit**

Even as a fellow event attendee, you can create great memories, if you dedicate quality time to others.

Go beyond the formal introduction, and share some personal stories and laughter.

You can also connect them with others you think could be a good fit (even if you met both of them just at that event). They will remember you as a leader and will want to give back.

## 34. Empathy is a networking superpower.

Putting yourself in the shoes of others (and walking in them) makes you a superstar in other people's eyes.

**How to make it a habit**

Make an experiment: try to see things with other people's eyes.

Do you have a feeling that someone is overwhelmed by the noise and the crowd?

Invite them to sit down in a quiet area and have a nice talk.

Do you see someone standing in a corner, too shy to walk to someone?

Invite them to join the conversation you have with others.

Have you read a post where someone shared an unfortunate turn in their career or life? Message them and offer support. Empathy makes you a better networker.

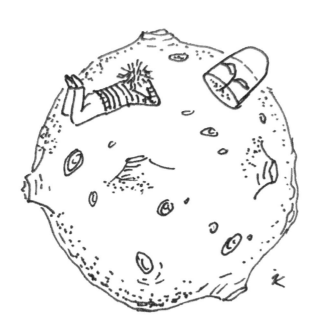

## 35. Don't nurture leads, build relationships with people.

Keeping in touch with people in a scheduled way with templated messages comes across as lead nurturing.

Let's be honest nobody wants to feel like a lead in someone's funnel.

**How to make it a habit**

Dedicate time each week to reaching out to a few of your connections without an agenda.

Ask how their children are - calling them by their names.

Check-in to see how their business, job is.

Recommend them on social media to your network.

Bayo Igoh, Business Coach has a habit of regularly WhatsApping connections asking how they are, without an agenda. It prompts people to do the same, a relationship is being born (which can even grow into a friendship).

## 36. Networking is not a series of pitches but an endless conversation with various people

Instead of talking about business and your achievements every time you meet others, concentrate on real conversations. Pick up on something they mentioned earlier about their hobbies, children, or pets and ask about that.

People are happy to share stories beyond business, and the whole relationship becomes more informal. It's ok to reveal more about yourself too, even if it is not related to business, it helps strengthen connections.

**How to make it a habit**

As you don't have endless time to have 1-2-1s with people, see how you can use other opportunities.

- If you attend a conference anyway, send the link to some of your connections who could be interested, and you might go together.
- If you visit a certain part of the town, or another place, publish a post to encourage connections to meet you.
- When you attend a networking event, organise 1-2-1s, or small group meetings before that.

## 37. Networking is a chance to make someone's life happier.

Connecting with others gives you an opportunity to brighten up their days.

Recognise them for an achievement.
Introduce them to someone.
Promote them in a post.
Involve them in a conversation.
Thank them for their advice.
Listen to their problems.
Or simply share laughter and a hug.

What an amazing power to bring sunshine to somebody else's life.

**How to make it a habit**
Introduce quick and easy habits of appreciation and recognition in your daily work:

- As you scroll your feed, congratulate those who announce good news (adding what you value in them).
- Message those who are in a difficult situation, offer help (and check in a few days later).
- Thank people (directly or in front of others).

38. If they don't understand, they won't remember. If they don't remember, they won't buy (and won't recommend you).

A lot of my network has a technical, or what they would describe 'boring' profession. (Myself included, think of 'marketing').

The more you can break it down for people to understand, the better.

Try to compare it to something they know. Bring examples of how you work.

**How to make it a habit**

Illustrate your profession with stories or use props like Miguel de Sousa Pires who brings an apple as he provides Apple Mac Support (genius!).

Always observe how people react. If you see
they are put off, you know you have to change
the way you explain it.

Listen to the questions they ask, and you can
adjust your pitch accordingly. You can also ask
them how they would explain it.

Fine-tune your pitch until it's easy to
understand for a 12-year-old (in a noisy room
full of other 12-year-olds:)

## 39. A strong network is like being on the cover of several magazines. Every day.

Having a strong network means a strong personal brand.

People talk about you and your strengths and successes even when you're not there.

People post about you, and tag you in posts and comments.
People recommend you to others, and introduce you to others.
People come to you saying that they follow you and are inspired by you.

You are in the minds of several people, some of them you don't even know.
It's like being on the cover of a magazine. Every day.

**How to make it a habit**

You can achieve this the easiest if you start elevating others.

One of the best things I did on LinkedIn was a Human Advent Calendar. From 1-24 December I featured one of my connections each day and introduced them to my network.

You don't have to do it for 24 days, but it's a good idea to dedicate 10-20% of your content to promoting others.

How you speak about others speaks about you.

You can tag them when you talk about a collaboration, you can give them a recommendation on LinkedIn, or give a public testimonial.

## 40. Different doesn't equal defective.

What I love about networking is that you come across all kinds of people, personalities, characters, cultures.

Not everybody behaves, talks, or dresses like you.

You might find people who do things differently, express themselves differently.

But - as long as their behaviour is appropriate - it's the beauty of it. It gives you an opportunity to get new insights and broaden your horizons.

**How to make it a habit**

Instead of always attending the same circles, experiment with completely new ones. Circles of completely different industries, professions and people.

I had fantastic insights - and awesome connections - attending circles of lawyers, artists, fashion designers, black entrepreneurs etc. (Always check if they accept people outside of their circles, most of the time they do.)

## 41. People you can count on count a lot in life.

You can get leads by advertising, and paying for coverage, but you can not buy people you can count on.

People you can count on to show up when they say they will.
Those who will support you when you are in pain,
who cheer for you when you are trying hard,
who celebrate with you when you succeed.

And these people count the most in life.

**How to make it a habit**

Think of the people who you can count on.
Send them a message or tell them how much you appreciate that they are there for you.

Send them a postcard without an agenda.
Invite them for lunch or coffee.
Ask them how you can help, what they are
working on.

It's never enough to recognise those who you
can count on and to show them they can count
on you too!

## 42. Selflessness sells.

*'She is such an adorable person, is always there for others.'*

*'He went above and beyond to help me, I'll never forget that.'*

People who help others without any agenda are talked about a lot.

It's something others will remember and share. On social media and in their network.

It's easy to say 'be selfless' but it's not always easy to do. Most people first think: *'What's in it for me?'*

**How to make it a habit**

Think of how you could go out of your way to support others. Niraj Kapur, LinkedIn and Sales Trainer regularly publishes posts to give a shoutout to books, podcasts, and professionals who he recommends.

Veshali Patel, Director of Pinnacle Advisory Services, Andy Wilkinson, Founder of OWB Creative, Yvonne Schimmel, Holistic Health Practitioner, Sarah Clay, LinkedIn Trainer always go above and beyond to give shoutout to others, and events they attend.

Jim McLaughlin, Owner of Estate Planning 4 Advisers and Membership Advisor of FSB, Stuart Moore, Radio 4Business, and Mark Orr, Printing and Direct Mail Expert make a regular effort to make valuable introductions.

## 43. Networking is a commitment. Not a campaign.

*'I have attended a few networking events, but nothing has come out of it.'*

*'I joined a networking group but it doesn't work for me.'*

*'I decided to message 3 people in my network every day, but no results yet.'*

Networking is not a performance campaign, where you can precisely target people, track results and optimise accordingly within a few months.

It's not a campaign you run and get hot leads out of it. (If you do, it's a nice plus, but it's not the default.)

It's a commitment to regularly attending the same circles (unless you totally dislike it) to be a familiar face.

A commitment to shouting out about others you have met to be liked.

A commitment to following up and doing what you promised to do to build trust.

**How to make it a habit**

- Start small, with a few people.
- Diarise meetings in advance, including follow up meetings.
- You can do some of the things right at the meeting (introducing people in email, sending over documents etc.)
- Book a few events in advance and stick to them.
- Don't stress yourself with being everywhere and meeting everybody.

44. Nobody cares about what your business does, but about who you care about.


Talk about who and what you care about instead of simply saying what your business does.
Talk about the cause you support and why.
Talk about what exactly care means to you (you can give examples).

Care is more than giving exceptional service (which is great in itself).

Care reaches much farther, way beyond client satisfaction.

It is about the transformation of lives, industries, places, and worlds through your services and activities.

**How to make it a habit**

Have you ever heard anybody saying *"We don't care at all about our clients."* Me neither.

This is why it doesn't make sense to say *"We care for our clients."*

Prepare some examples of what care means, how it looks. It's not only about clients, but your team, suppliers, connections and causes.

## 45. The best networking doesn't feel like working.

*'How can you do so many networking events?'* - people ask me.

*'Networking can be so exhausting, I'm taking a break now.'* - say some others.

The fact is that if anyone feels networking is tiring, overwhelming, or exhausting, doesn't do real networking.

What they do is rushing to events, stressing about talking to the 'important people', collecting connections, and pitching to everyone.

I agree it's draining.

What I mean by networking is different.

It's hearing inspiring stories.

Sharing the success of others.

Getting to know their background, family, and friends.

Being invited to incredible places.

Being the one they trust when things go south.

Celebrating with others.

Being with nice people.

And being with nice people is never tiring.

## How to make it a habit

If you ever feel you're overwhelmed by networking, the best thing is to list all the things you do as part of your networking.

What are the ones you are doing only as 'an obligation' because you already paid for it, already committed, or because you think it will be beneficial?

Try to find the reason why you find these overwhelming. Is it the frequency of the meetings? The people? Is it too far from you? Is it that you don't see any return from it? What do you miss if you stop doing it?

If you can't change the disturbing factor, it's ok to stop doing some of the activities - or pause them - even if you think these can be beneficial. Doing networking (or anything) which you dislike, won't be beneficial for you as a whole.

On the other hand, keep those which you really like. Where you can build meaningful relationships, even if you haven't seen a financial or business return. Enjoying something is in itself a return, and eventually you still build relationships.

## 46. You can get everything if you ask for it.

Some people need to learn to give first.
Some people need to learn to ask when they need help.

When you have done enough watering, it's time to be the garden - as the saying goes.

If you always tell everyone that business is awesome, your training course/event/whatever is selling out (while it's not), people won't know they should help.

We talk a lot about giving first, but there's also a time to ask.

**How to make it a habit**

Think of the people you have helped in the past year.

It's ok to message connections and ask for help:

"Can you think of someone who would be interested in this and this?'

"Can you give me 30 minutes of your time to help me with your feedback?"

"I need 10 more signups, could you reach out to your network?"

"Business is not what I expected this year, can we brainstorm on what could be done?"

People might or might not help (many of them will).

But if you expect them to notice something is wrong and find it out themselves (while your

social media says you do awesome), there's a
very low chance they will.

## 47. Networking is not about collecting contacts. It's about respecting relations.

'*I have 10,000 connections on LinkedIn.*'

'*I'm working the room, I want to talk to everybody.*'

'*I need to talk to about 8-10 quality people per event.*'

People who say these sentences collect connections.
It's easy.
You can scan LinkedIn profiles, and exchange business cards after a few minutes of talk.

But these connections are not relationships. They won't remember you, won't talk about you, they won't recommend you. (And honestly, neither will you.)

**How to make it a habit**

Give more time to exchanging thoughts before exchanging contact details.

I always make a photo of the business card/LinkedIn profile/Connection details, and later make some notes on the photo. I have a document to keep all the info in one place.

Schedule time to follow up (regularly), and to give support you committed to.
Don't cancel networking catch up meetings unless absolutely necessary, and even then schedule another.
Respect the person and the relationship with them.

## 48. Build your reputation by helping others build theirs.

People who start their business or career, often find it hard to build their reputation.

'*What can I talk about?*'
'*I hate talking about myself.*' - they say.

Good news! There's no need to talk only about yourself to build your reputation.
Start talking about others to build theirs.

**How to make it a habit**

Dedicate a certain percentage of your content to others when planning your content calendar.

- Featuring brilliant businesses.
- Thanking people publicly for their outstanding service.

- Promoting their events, courses, and product launches.
- Being involved in fundraising campaigns.

Not only on social media, but in email newsletters and direct messages.

'*I really like how you always help others.*' - I get this feedback a lot. When you talk about others, it talks about you.

## 49. Generous is not an adjective, it's an attitude.

I get a lot of messages offering 'help' to do my social media content, to generate leads and many others. These are sales pitches, and in their case 'help' means a paid service.

Some people say *"I help XYZ, they have a lot of high net worth connections, this could be good for me later."*

Just to make it clear: being generous with strings attached, is not being generous. It's building a business funnel.

Being generous is doing it without an agenda. It can take many shapes and forms discussed above, from listening to someone to connecting them to a business opportunity.

And it definitely includes supporting causes and people in need via charities, fundraisers, group and individual initiatives.

## How to make it a habit

Many of my connections commit a certain amount of time, and budget every month to help charities. I find it has a more long term impact than ad hoc donations. It also helps me say 'No.' to some other requests which would be too overwhelming for my schedule (or to those people who can afford paying me).

When I see that someone runs a fundraising campaign, I donate a smaller amount - something I would spend on lunch or drinks, and I give publicity to the cause.

Our networking organisations support charitable causes and we give free access to our events to charities.

## 50. Networking. Always. Works.

There will always be events which are a waste of your time.
1-2-1s which are more like...ones.
People you invested time and energy in who simply disappear when you need them.

But in the long run, networking always works.

If I had to choose to give you my money or my network, I'd give you my money without hesitating for a second.

My network would help me rebuild my fortune, but no fortune could buy my network.

**Make networking a habit.**

Thank you for reading the book.

Now it's time to practice things. If you want to try yourself, come to one of our London Business Society events organised at prestigious places in London.

We have around 80 business leaders, CEOs, professionals at each event from many industries. Attendees can get to know each other in the WhatsApp group prior to the event, and we have a hosting team on site to facilitate introductions.

See the details here (linkedin.com/company/business-club-london/), or email me: tk@franciscooper.com.

See you soon,

Timea

Printed in Great Britain
by Amazon